Village in Nigeria

Text and photographs by Carol Barker

Adam and Charles Black · London

My name is Thaddeus and I'm twelve years old. Here I am with my parents. I live with my family in the village of Aye-Ekan. This is in Kwara state in the south-west of Nigeria. The nearest town to us is Omu-Aran. It's only eleven kilometres away and we can go there by bus.

My father is a farmer, like most people in our village. His name is Chief Afolayan. He's one of several chiefs who help to run the village.

This is our home in Aye-Ekan. We live in two houses on one side of the compound and my uncle, Anthony Fas, and his family live on the other side. The compound is like a big yard with the houses grouped around it. It is called 'ode-ede', which means 'the most suitable place'.

We are Yoruba people and speak the Yoruba language. There are four main groups of people in Nigeria. We Yoruba are the largest group in the south. Then there are the Hausa and Fulani people in the north, and the Ibo people in the east.

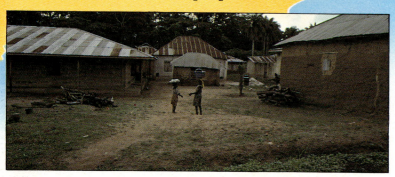

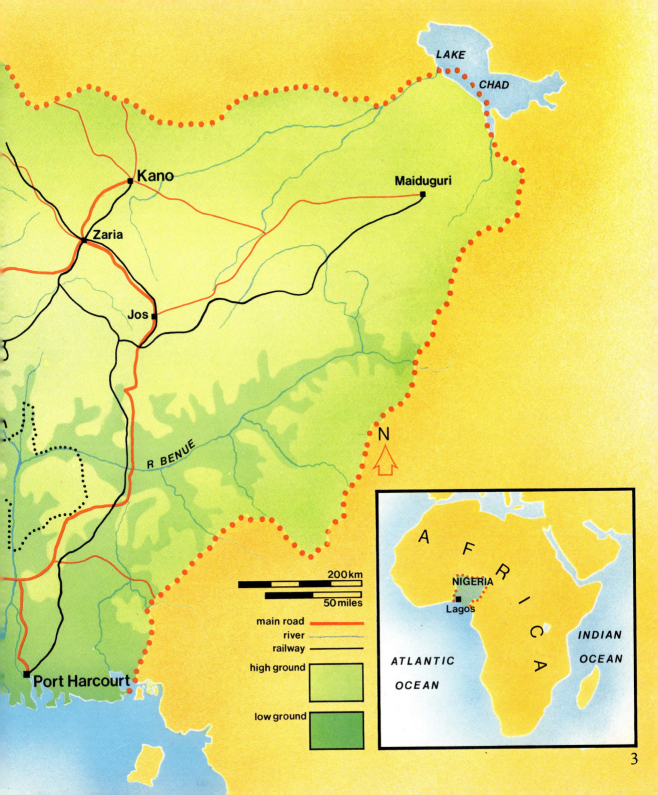

LAKE
CHAD

Kano

Maiduguri

Zaria

Jos

R BENUE

N

Port Harcourt

200 km

50 miles

main road
river
railway
high ground

low ground

AFRICA

NIGERIA
Lagos

ATLANTIC
OCEAN

INDIAN
OCEAN

3

My mother's name is Aransi. Here we are with my father and some of our family and friends. We're a big family because my father has six wives. Most of the men in our village have two wives. But my father has three senior wives and three junior wives. Aransi is his third wife. There are sixteen children in our family but some of them have grown up and moved to other places.

This is Maria, the fourth wife. She's looking after one of the babies. My mother and the other senior wives teach the younger wives how to look after the children.

The women in our family have a lot of work to do, besides looking after the babies. All our water for cooking and drinking comes from a river about two kilometres away. The women have to carry the water home in buckets. They also collect wood from the forest and chop it up to make fires for cooking.

We older children help the women to prepare and cook the food. Today, it's my brother Peter's turn to peel and wash the yams. When they are peeled, the yams will be boiled and pounded into a mash. My mother says yams are very good for you. We eat them almost every day – for breakfast lunch or supper. Tonight we'll have them with a hot vegetable soup made of okra (ladies' fingers), chilli peppers and red palm nut oil. You can also eat yams with maize (corn-on-the-cob), beans or green vegetables.

5

This is Elizabeth, the first wife. She's the most important person in the family, after my father. On some days, she sits outside our house and sells bread, red peppers and flour made from the cassava plants which grow on our farm.

Elizabeth and the other wives all try to earn some extra money besides the money we earn from our farm produce.

Every four days, there is a market at Aye-Ekan. My mother likes to go with the other two senior wives. When ever she can, she will take some cassava flour or ground nuts to sell. During the school holidays I go with her and help carry her baskets.

Markets are very important in Nigeria. They are all organised and run by women. I love going because there's so much to see. There are live birds sold in baskets, all kinds of vegetables, like maize and red peppers, nuts, yams, also sugar cane, bananas, palm wine in casks, meat, fish and brightly coloured cloth. You can even buy live snails or tortoises! There is something for everyone.

Sometimes, my mother takes one of the junior wives to visit the Health Centre in Aye-Ekan. It's open every Thursday for women to bring their babies for health and weight checks, or vaccinations.

When I was three months old, my mother brought me here and I was vaccinated against diseases like polio, measles, whooping cough, diphtheria and tuberculosis.

The Health Centre was built in 1963, with funds raised by our people. There is always a dispenser there, and doctors and nurses come to visit on different days of each week. People who are very ill go to the hospital at Omu-Aran.

My father is a traditional doctor and herbalist. He treats sick people with herbs and traditional medicines.

At first, he did not believe in modern medicines. He wouldn't allow his senior wives to take their children to the Health Centre. My mother wasn't allowed to take my eldest brother, Abiodun, there. But some of my brothers and sisters died of diseases like polio. So my father realised that his traditional medicines could not cure them. Then he allowed Aransi to take me to the Health Centre.

People still come to my father for treatment and he still believes in herbal medicine. He says that traditional and modern medicines should work together to cure the sick.

On Sundays, I go to St. Michael's Catholic Church
in Aye-Ekan, with some of my brothers and sisters.
My uncle, Anthony Fas, is assistant to the Roman
Catholic priest. When the Reverend Father is away
on leave in Europe, my uncle takes the church
service on Sunday mornings. I am standing next to
him with some of the other children before we
go to church.

When I was a baby, I was baptized in St. Michael's. I've always been brought up as a Catholic. My younger brothers and sisters are all Catholics, too. So are the junior wives. My father and mother still follow the Yoruba gods. So do the other senior wives and the eldest children.

This means that half our family follow the Yoruba religion and half are Christian. We are quite happy all living together and don't quarrel about it. My uncle says Aye-Ekan is just the same, with about half the people following Yoruba gods and half following the Christian religion. Most of the Christians are Roman Catholics. There are some Muslim people in Aye-Ekan, too. They worship in the mosque at Aye-Ekan. But there are many more Muslims in Northern Nigeria than there are where I live.

In the old days, Yoruba people worshipped 420 gods and goddesses. But now, only the main ones are worshipped.

First in the Yoruba religion comes Olodumare, the Creator. All the others gods and goddesses are under him They are called Orishas (lesser gods). All the gods, except for Olodumare, have their own priests and their own festivals. The most important is the God Ifa of Divination. His priests are diviners, called Babalawo. They tell people's fortunes.

This man is wearing an Epa mask. He's with the chief Epa priest. The Epa festival is to worship the God of Wood and also for the spirits of our ancestors. People believe that these spirits enter into the masks as the men are dancing.

One of the biggest festivals is for Oshun, Goddess of the River. It's held every year at Oshogbo, near the town where the river Oshun flows. Thousands of people come to the sacred grove to worship the Goddess Oshun. There are drummers and trumpeters and a lot of dancing. Oshun is the Goddess of Fertility. Women pray to her for children. People also pray for prosperity and collect sacred water from the river Oshun.

My mother Aransi, is a priestess of Obatala, the god who carves and moulds human beings before they are born. Aransi is a leader in the festival for Obatala. My father follows the God Osanyin of Medicine, as he is a traditional doctor.

This is George Bamedele Arowogun. He's a master woodcarver and he's carving a male Epa mask for the Epa festival. Woodcarvers like George are called Onishona (people who make art). They carve masks and figures for the Yoruba gods and goddesses and for shrines and festivals.

Woodcarving is a very important job. It's only done by men and it takes a long time to learn. George started learning when he was ten years old. He trained under a master woodcarver until he was twenty-six. Now, George has his own assistant to train.

George spent the first fifteen years of his career travelling around and making carvings for Yoruba festivals and shrines. He made Epa masks, Ogboni drums, warriors on horseback, hunters, women worshipping the Goddess Oshun and many ceremonial objects. Then Father Kevin Carroll, a Roman Catholic priest, saw his work. He liked it so much that he asked George to do some woodcarvings for the Catholic Church.

This is a scene showing the Three Kings bringing gifts to the baby Jesus, and Mary. It is part of the carved wooden doors which George made for the church at Osi-Illorin.

Now, George carves for the Catholic Church as well as the Yoruba religion. He says it doesn't worry him. But when George became a Christian he stopped believing that the spirits of gods lived in the Yoruba masks and figures.

15

There are some other special jobs for men in our villages. There's a blacksmith, a carpenter and a cobbler. In Aye-Ekan, people make almost everything they need – from building houses to making clothes.

Some special crafts, like weaving, are only for women. The mothers teach their daughters.

Afolabi, my father's fifth wife, is very good at weaving. She works on a loom in our house.

Today, she's weaving plain yellow cloth, but she can weave all kinds of different colours and patterns. When she has finished, Afolabi takes the cloth to a tailor who lives nearby. The tailor has a sewing machine and he makes the cloth into clothes for our family.

My mum weaves cloth sometimes and so do all the other wives. They take it in turns, in between their other work.

Pottery is another craft which only women do. This is Mrs Adeola Babaola. She has taught her daughter how to make pots and the two of them always work together.

The pots are made of clay and dried in the sun. They're baked in a fire at the back of the house so they will be hard and strong. Then the pots are covered in liquid from locust beans, to make them black and shiny.

Mrs Babaola and her daughter make pots of all different sizes. There are big pots for storing water or cooking yams, right down to tiny pots for storing medicine. The pots are sold in the market at Aye-Ekan and people come from miles away to buy them.

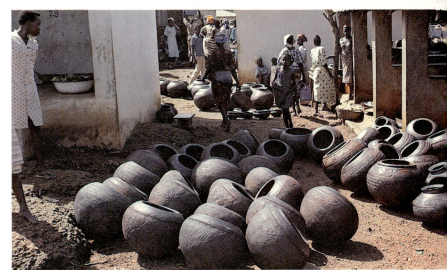

I don't live in Aye-Ekan all the time. My father owns two houses. Our main family house, with two acres of land, is at Aye-Ekan. The smaller farm house is in the forest and has four acres of land.

During the school term I live at Aye-Ekan, but during the holidays I always go to the farm house to help with the farm work. It's about twenty five kilometres from Aye-Ekan, near the village of Alariasa. We take the bus for sixteen kilometres and then walk the rest of the way through the forest.

I like living on the farm. When I'm not working in the fields or helping in the house, I can play and do what I like. I've made a catapult, called 'kanna-kanna', and I can shoot squirrels, birds and bushrats with it.

My father says he's getting too old for hard work, so my eldest brother, Andrew, is in charge of most of the farm work. Andrew and his family live here almost all the time. So do my father's youngest wives, Afolabi and Kolajo. They look after the children, fetch water and firewood and cook the food. Today, I'm helping Kolajo to pound the yams for lunch.

We grow all the vegetables that we need on the farm. The main crops are yams, maize and cassava. We also grow vegetables like okra, peppers, tomatoes and green vegetables. Banana trees, oil-palm trees and kola-nut trees grow on the farm, too.

My brothers and I help on the farm from Monday to Saturday, with a rest on Sunday. The work we do depends on the time of year. We help with weeding, planting yams, or harvesting the yams and maize. The yams grow as tall vines, but you can only eat the tubers (like huge potatoes) which grow under the ground.

We have two main seasons in Yorubaland. The rainy season lasts from mid-March to September. The dry season lasts from October to mid-March. During the rainy season the weeds in the yam plots grow very fast, so we spend a lot of time weeding. My father works with us most of the time. There aren't any tractors or machines on the farm. We use a cutlass (a long wide knife), or a hoe for most jobs.

My father has six acres of land altogether. But he doesn't farm all six acres at once. He grows crops on one part of the land for two years. Then that part is left to rest, or lie fallow, for a year. During this time, my father has to use another part of his land. He also clears new areas of forest for growing crops. After a year, he can go back to using the first plot of land. This is called crop rotation.

At the end of the holidays, I go back to Aye-Ekan and get ready for school. Here I am in my school uniform, with my brother Raphael and my cousin Patrick. It takes us about half an hour to walk to school.

We go to St. Michael's Roman Catholic Primary School. Only Catholic children are allowed to go there. There's another school for Muslim children in the village.

There is also a school which is run by the government. This school hadn't been built when my mother and father were young. They weren't allowed to go to the Catholic school, so they never learned to read or write.

When I was born, my mother and father decided that I should be christened so that I could go to St. Michael's School. I started at the school in Class One, when I was six years old. This year, I'm in Class Six

There aren't any lessons for the first few days of school. The boys cut the long grass with cutlasses and the girls weed the paths. Then we move the desks and chairs into the right classrooms. Lessons only start properly on the following Monday.

I like it at school. We learn English, Arithmetic, Health Education, General Knowledge, Bible, Yoruba, Nature Study, Art and Social Studies, including History and Geography. But my favourite subject is Arithmetic. I enjoy doing calculation.

Our teacher, Mr Alufa, was born here in Aye-Ekan. But he's travelled all over Nigeria. He shows us pictures of all the places he has been to. When he was training to be a teacher Mr Alufa lived in Lagos, the capital city of Nigeria. Lagos is a big modern city on the south coast, a long way from our village.

Mr Alufa says that Lagos was too crowded and busy, so he came back to Aye-Ekan to teach. He says that most of the people in Nigeria used to be farmers like us. But during the 1960s and 1970s, more and more oil was found in our country. People started to work in the oil industry, instead of farming.

24

Now, Nigeria sells a lot of oil to other countries. It has become one of the richest countries in Africa. But there aren't enough people working on the land like us. Nigeria has to buy food and other goods from different countries. This is expensive, so the price of food and clothes has gone up a lot, even in Aye-Ekan. Most of the people who earn high wages live in towns and oil doesn't seem to help us farmers in the country.

I like living in Aye-Ekan. But when I'm older, I'd like to go to the University of Lagos to become a clerk and work in an office. My father and mother hope that I might be a doctor or an engineer. They'd like me to do something different from farming. But my mother says she doesn't really mind what I choose to do, as long as I am happy.

Barker, Carol
Village in Nigeria.—(Beans)
1. Nigeria—Social life and custom—Juvenile
literature
I. Title
966.9'05   DT515.4

ISBN 0–7136–2391–8

A & C Black (Publishers) Limited
35 Bedford Row, London WC1R 4JH

© 1984 Carol Barker
The map is by Tony Garrett

ISBN 0-7136-2391-8

Filmset by August Filmsetting, Warrington, Cheshire
Colour origination by Hongkong Graphic Arts Service Centre, Hong Kong
Printed in Great Britain by Hazell Watson and Viney Ltd. Aylesbury, Bucks